HOW TO GET RICH
ON THE
OREGON TRAIL

MY ADVENTURES AMONG COWS, CROOKS & HEROES ON THE ROAD TO FAME AND FORTUNE

If the family makes the journey west, you will need a place to record your experiences. Do not forget your grandfather when you make your first fortune as a writer.

S. R.

WRITING JOURNAL OF:

Master William Reed

PORTLAND, OREGON
1852

GIFT OF MR. SILAS REED

NATIONAL GEOGRAPHIC

WASHINGTON, D.C.

March 23, 2004

To the editors of National Geographic:

My great-grandfather, William Reed, was a legend in our family. He traveled the world for some 70 years, reporting on everything from the Opium Wars in China to the discovery of King Tut's tomb. His travels became the material for grandiloquent orations at the dinner table that apparently held my grandfather and his siblings in thrall for hours.

For all his adventures, the stories my great-grandfather most liked to tell came from his experiences in a wagon train during the great westward migration on the Oregon Trail. He was just 15 at the time, but already an accomplished writer. On this, the 80th anniversary of his death, I dug through many dusty volumes of his old journals and found the remarkable pages that I enclose in this package.

William's journal is a record of anticipation and excitement, of fear and struggle for survival, of hope for a life of opportunity. He records the perils of the journey with amazing wit and immediacy. Cattle rustlers and scam artists, Indian traders and trail guides, mountain men and preachers, all come to life in these pages. To illustrate his adventure, William pasted into his journal images from the time, as well as his own drawings. He also kept a careful record of the family's finances, under the watchful eye of my great-great-grandmother.

Please consider William's journal for publication. It was his final wish that these pages should find their way into print.

Yours,

Amanda Reed

Amanda Reed

EDITOR'S NOTE:
Try as we may, we at National Geographic have not been able to locate Ms. Amanda Reed. Nor have we found a single semi-colon of William Reed's supposedly prolific writings outside of the pages of this journal. While the journal's account of life on the Oregon Trail is as accurate as any history text (and quite a lot more fun), it should be read with an attitude of skeptical inquiry. For an assessment of the facts contained in these pages, written with just such an attitude, see the afterword following Mr. Reed's journal.

SELF-PORTRAIT
BY WILLIAM REED

The author himself, depicted as a typical emigrant on the Oregon Trail. Taken from the pages of his journal and annotated by the 15-year-old Mr. Reed.

Pots and pans (in the hope that we will actually have something to put in them)

Blacksmith's hammer (thanks to my brother, for fixing wagon wheels and other casualties of the trail)

Flour (avoid dunking at all costs)

Extra shirt and pants, for use after the latest dunking

Buffalo chips, to burn for fuel

Sturdy boots (2,000 miles is a long way, and the wagon carries more important things; pickles for instance)

Pen and ink (significantly lighter than a hammer and in my opinion more powerful)

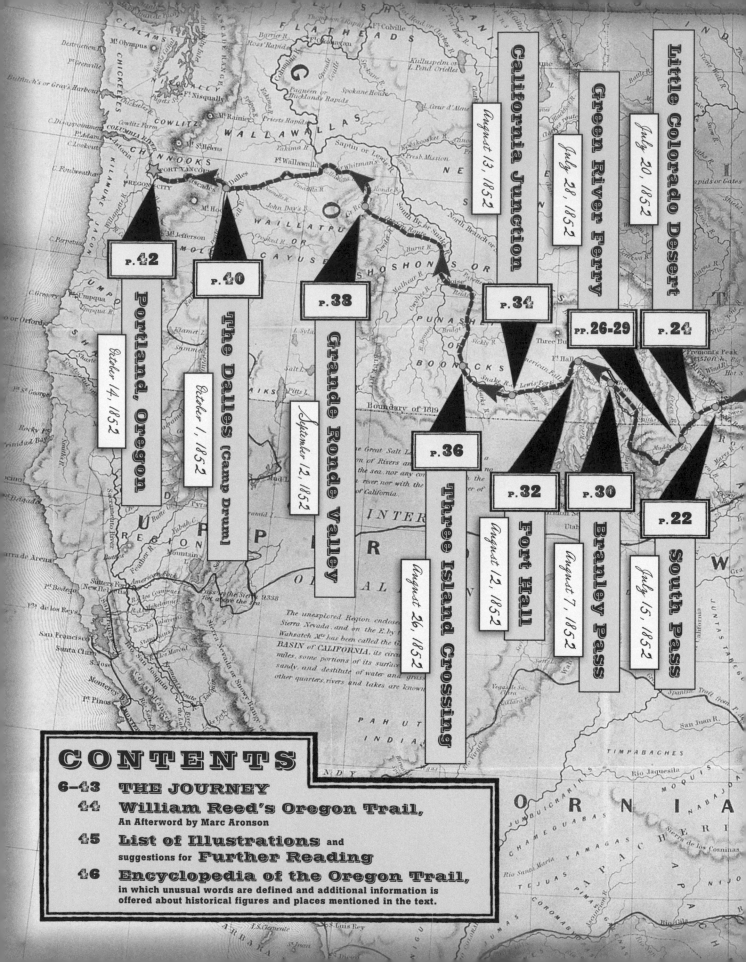

Little Colorado Desert
July 20, 1852
p.24

Green River Ferry
July 28, 1852
pp.26-29

California Junction
August 13, 1852
p.34

Portland, Oregon
October 14, 1852
p.42

The Dalles (Camp Drum)
October 1, 1852
p.40

Grande Ronde Valley
September 12, 1852
p.38

Three Island Crossing
August 26, 1852
p.36

Fort Hall
August 12, 1852
p.32

Bradley Pass
August 7, 1852
p.30

South Pass
July 15, 1852
p.22

CONTENTS

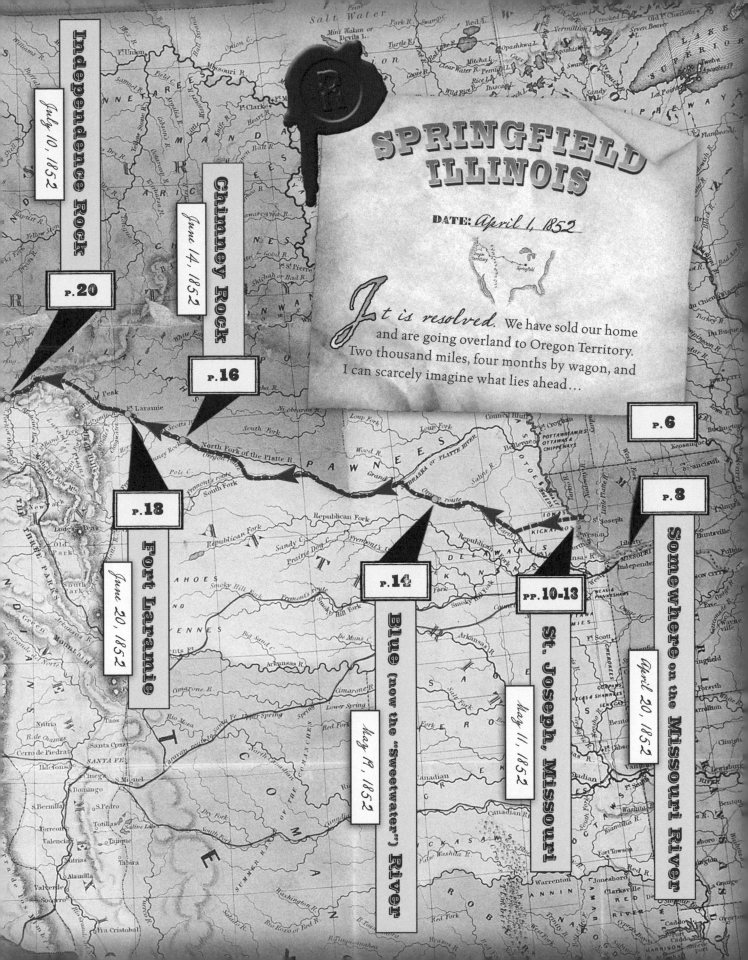

Independence Rock
July 10, 1852
p. 20

Chimney Rock
June 14, 1852
p. 16

SPRINGFIELD ILLINOIS

DATE: *April 1, 1852*

It is resolved. We have sold our home and are going overland to Oregon Territory. Two thousand miles, four months by wagon, and I can scarcely imagine what lies ahead…

p. 6

p. 8

Fort Laramie
June 20, 1852
p. 18

Blue (now the "Sweetwater") River
May 19, 1852
p. 14

St. Joseph, Missouri
May 11, 1852
pp. 10-13

Somewhere on the Missouri River
April 20, 1852

SPRINGFIELD ILLINOIS

Abraham Lincoln served our state government as a congressman here. I consider him my friend, as my father treated him once for melancholia.

It is resolved. We have sold our home and are going overland to Oregon Territory. Two thousand miles, four months by wagon, and I can scarcely imagine what lies ahead. Father cannot contain his excitement. "In coin, we are neither rich nor poor, but live in relative comfort," he told us all at supper last night, conducting an imaginary orchestra with his knife. "But it is not in our nature to be content with comfort. Your great-grandfather crossed the broad ocean from Scotland to Massachusetts to find fields expansive enough for his dreams. Your grandfather journeyed from Massachusetts to Illinois to educate the youth of our new frontier. Your forebears followed the siren call of opportunity ever westward, and now our time has come. Oregon brims with unclaimed land, with emigrants hopeful for the future and needful of our services. And so we set out into the wilderness, knowing not from whence our next meal will come…" I remember little after that but the anxious clatter of forks as we sought to fill ourselves with nourishment before preparing to set off into the land of opportunity.

MY PRIVATE FEARS

I am excited, for every writer needs inspiration, and more than a few have gotten it miles from home. But I am scared, and I do not mind confessing my fears for our journey.

☞ **Starvation** (I am fond of eating and do not wish to give it up)

☞ **Thirst** (we will be crossing the Great American Desert)

☞ **Death** by drowning (how is it that we must ford rivers by the score in order to cross the desert?)

☞ **Indians** (the skin atop my head has served me well these 15 years, keeping the sun off my brain and all that)

My family and traveling companions

As a journalist, I have interviewed each of them about their hopes and dreams for our new life in the West.

My elder brother, Nathan Reed

TRADE: **APPRENTICE BLACKSMITH**

"Why, to make my fortune. In Oregon, a blacksmith is worth the weight of his anvil in gold."

My mother, Eliza Reed

TRADE: **MANAGER OF JOHN REED**

"My hope is that your father's dreams do not make us paupers."

My elder sister, Abigail Reed

TRADE: **QUEEN OF FAMILY**

"I speak only to real journalists."

My father, John Reed

TRADE: **PHYSICIAN**

(I have more than adequately recorded his thoughts.)

My grandfather, Silas Reed

TRADE: **SCHOOLMASTER**

"I'm sorry, Will, but my traveling days are done."

Me, William Reed

TRADE: **WRITER**

As for me, I append this letter from the editor of our newspaper here in Springfield.

Dear Mr. William Reed,

I would be pleased to receive your letters from the trail and to consider them for publication. Our readers are eager for news from the West.

Sincerely,

Mr. Allen Francis

Illinois State Journal

SOMEWHERE ON THE MISSOURI RIVER

DATE: *April 20, 1852*

This is James Marsden and "his" negro, Joseph. Though the slave state, Missouri, is our neighbor, I have never before seen a man who has been bought and sold like a head of cattle.

The day may come when I stand on solid ground, but I do not know when. We were a week on the road to St. Louis in a coach that still contains three of my teeth, rattled by turns out of my head. We now sway and lurch aboard a steamboat so large it suggests they have discovered how to make a city float (like the one I am pasting in here). On the upper deck, there are 700 tons of wagons, pig (dead and smoked), cattle (alive, to judge from the smell), and more. All of it is bound for the West. Have not yet seen an Indian, but it is said that they are set to trade places with us and move east. They have seen so many people going the other way that they wonder how there can be any white people left in the States. We are to travel in company with others for mutual aid and protection. My father has enlisted fellow travelers on the boat. I have sketched here three of his more questionable choices.

This preening fellow is called Byron Strong. I don't care for him, but Abigail does. She will have to beware his father, Ezra, who is a preacher. If God is as stern as he is, we are all in trouble.

Mother says that in my journal I am to keep a record of our transactions along the way for she does not want to go broke getting to the land of opportunity.

I am told that our steamboat cost $50,000 to make but that the owner will make it back in a single season.

LEDGER

DATE:	April 1-20
BEGINNING BALANCE:	
Savings, sale of house:	$1,850.00
INCOME:	$0
EXPENSES:	
Stagecoach, Springfield to St. Louis ($8/passenger):	$40.00
Meals:	$75.00
Steamboat, St. Louis to St. Joe ($12/passenger & $12 freight):	$72.00
CURRENT BALANCE:	$1,663.00

This man calls himself *Stannard*. He says he has a nose for gold and struck it rich on the stuff in California. He is bound for Green River, where he opened a trading post with his profits.

St. Joseph, Missouri

April 28, 1852

Here is the last outpost of civilization, where the entire population of the United States is outfitting itself before setting off for the West.

Our company now numbers 66 people and 14 wagons.

We met a man who is set on driving 2,000 turkeys to Oregon. He bought them at 50 cents a head and says he will sell them for $8 when he arrives.

Grist mills turn out flour by the ton for the emigrants. I aim to be sure we have enough for pie.

MISSOURI MILLS

We saw several "Bloomer costumes." Nathan wondered if they have invented a third sex, between male and female. For his wit he received a blow to the head from Abigail.

Blacksmiths like this one make last-minute repairs to a battalion of wagons. Nathan claims we could make our fortune on the trail if we were not in such a hurry to get to Oregon.

I have survived my first encounter with the Indians, who mingle in the streets without anyone marking it strange. Some have rifles and are dressed no differently from a white man.

JOES TACK

DEEDS

HOTEL

HARDWARE BLACKSMITH

UIS FEEDS

Stannard prowls the town, crowing about his knowledge of the West. He sells maps—"only" $50—to a lake in California that is supposedly full of gold.

ST. JOSEPH MISSOURI

DATE: *May 11, 1852*

Our Purchases

4 yoke oxen	$280.00

(I have named them Lincoln, Clay, Garrison, Washington, Jefferson, Adams, Cooper, & Irving.)

2 Milk cows	80.00
1 Donkey	50.00
1 Wagon	150.00
3 Rifles	60.00
Lead, 30 lbs.	1.50
Powder, 25 lbs.	5.50
Flour, 1,000 lbs.	150.00
Bacon, 450 lbs.	60.00
Coffee, 25 lbs.	12.50
Tea, 5 lbs.	2.75
Sugar, 125 lbs.	67.50
Pickles, one barrel, 20 lbs.	10.00
Dried fruit, 50 lbs.	3.00
Salt, pepper, &c., 50 lbs.	3.00
Lard, 50 lbs.	2.50
Saleratus, 10 lbs	1.00
Cooking utensils, 30 lbs.	4.00
Tent, 30 lbs.	5.00
Bedding, 45 lbs.	22.50
Matches	1.00
Candles and soap	7.00
Clothes, tools, etc., 230 lbs.	0

(brought from home)

Total ..... 2,175 lbs. $978.75

"How much for saleratus!?" "Why did you spend so dearly on the bacon? I could have had it for 20 cents to the pound." "An entire barrel of pickles!? Dear, we will sink into the plains."

Mother's preachings have nearly made me long for Father's speeches, but he has been silenced by the strain of preparations. I think that Mother secretly believes that we are foolish to trade a decent life for something completely unknown. But she is a practical person and once committed to a course of action, wants to see it through in the best way possible. She is eager to leave St. Joe, and so am I. The merchants here sell their goods at one price to local residents and reserve their highest prices for the emigrants. Our trail guidebook (30 cents) tells us that the smart traveler will be on the plains by May 1 or risk being trapped in the early snows at the western mountains. Still, we cannot leave. The Indians say that the prairie grasses are late this year and our cattle will have nothing to eat. So we wait. Mother has spent four days now checking her list with our pile of supplies.

I saw an amazing contraption very much like this one as we passed Independence, 20 miles downriver. It was invented by a man called Wind-Wagon Thomas, who claims he can make 15 miles per hour across the prairie with a good breeze.

12

Our Chariot

We store valuables here for safekeeping.

False floor. We store provisions beneath it and sleep on top, though I think I will prefer to sleep under the stars.

This is called the "tongue." Mother has given strict orders to stay clear of it while we are moving.

Rub the wagon bed with tar and it will float— or, so they claim.

Wheels must be greased daily with lard from a buffalo or other unfortunate creature.

Rope, water, grease buckets, spare spokes, and my sister (if necessary) will be stored here.

Mr. Ox for President?

There is so much impassioned debate here over which animal is best suited to pull us to Oregon that one would think we are debating the future leadership of our country. And so, I ask, who is to be the next president of these United States: Mr. Ox, Mr. Mule, or Mr. Horse?

	FOR	AGAINST
OX	✵ Strong ✵ Durable ✵ Dumb enough to pull 2,500 pounds across a continent without protest ✵ Considers prairie grass a delicacy	✵ Spooks easily ✵ Tends to stampede for water
MULE	✵ Fast ✵ Enjoys cottonwood bark when grass is not on the menu	✵ Stubborn and brutish ✵ Not as strong as Mr. Ox
HORSE	✵ Very fast	✵ Often stolen by Sioux or other Indians ✵ Not very strong ✵ Not durable

LEDGER

DATE:	April 20–May 11
BEGINNING BALANCE:	$1,663.00
INCOME:	$0
EXPENSES: Supplies (see list):	$978.75
CURRENT BALANCE:	$684.25

BLUE
(NOW THE "SWEETWATER") RIVER

DATE: *May 19, 1852*

We are on the trail at last, yet Mother is not happy. The churning rivers have got us already, and she must make a new list. Here is how it happened: Seven days out from St. Joseph, we reached the Big Blue. The water was low, and many in our company wanted to ford as we could easily walk the oxen across. Father felt it safer to take the ferry and negotiated a fair price of $1.50 a wagon. We camped the night, and when we woke, rain had come and swelled the river. Seeing that we could not cross by ourselves if we wanted to, the ferryman raised his price to $3. Father was willing to pay it, but "Mr. Master" (Mr. Marsden) refused and had a scrap with the ferryman, whereby several men appeared with rifles to emphasize the fairness of the fee. After much debate, it was decided to move on and find a place to ford. And that was our error. Halfway across, Lincoln lost his footing, and the rest of the team went with him. We lost half our flour to the river and all our sugar. Our guidebook tells us the Sweetwater River is still 500 miles distant, but given the way we have sweetened this river, I have borrowed its name for the Big Blue.

We have passed 14 new made graves, and father is worried for us. He has already treated several people for the measles and for cholera.

Poles (like the one this boatman wields) *are important at river crossings—if used wisely. It was Nathan's job to cross first, test for quicksand, and plant poles where the ground was SUPPOSEDLY firm.*

From my friend J. Goldsborough Bruff, who preceded me on the trail by three years. He chose the gold fields over Oregon, but returned home rich only in memories, which he committed to paper with an expert eye.

Here are the two other choices for *river crossings*, neither of them good. Ferries are often makeshift rafts made of logs, canoes, or wagon beds lashed together. Most bridges are as perilous as the one Bruff drew here. Some are run by Indians. The Sac and Fox, for example, have a bridge at Wolf Creek. We paid them $1 a wagon and 25 cents an animal to cross.

Taken from the E. bank

Perilous ferriage of the Missouri, 7 miles below old Ft. Kearny, June 1, 2, 3, & 4th - 1849, (during a great freshet)

above St. Joseph

Nathan insists we would earn more than $5,000 if we settled for the summer and built our own bridge. His plea seemed to interest Mother, but Father would hear nothing of it.

Bruff May 23d 1849

CHIMNEY ROCK

DATE: *June 14, 1852*

RIP SALLY

*T*he cholera has us in its grip, and the Platte River is littered with broken dreams. Still we press on, the entire population of the country rolling through the dust to its grave. It is a terrible disease, and I have intimate knowledge of it, as I have been helping Father treat patients up and down the trail. It begins with diarrhea, then turns to cramps in the stomach and legs, and finally to vomiting. It results in death for half the people we treat. Father does not know what causes it but says its victims seem to have drunk bad water or breathed noxious air. Mr. Strong is more certain. He says it is God's vengeance for our sins, though I do not understand why God would have chosen the five-year-old girl with the blonde plaits who died yesterday. She could not yet have done anything to warrant such a punishment. Her family tore boards from their wagon to build her a proper coffin.

Cholera Morbus

is about as sure to come as Summer is. It comes suddenly and without warning — is Dangerous and often Fatal. **Are You Prepared** for it's coming? If any of your family are attacked "PROMPT action only may save life. For **46 YEARS** ONE medicine has ALWAYS cured Cholera, Cholera Morbus Diarrhoea, Dysentery and all SUMMER COMPLAINTS *children* can take it with perfect safety. This medicine is **Perry Davis' Pain Killer.** To be on the safe side get some NOW and have it on hand. For sale by all Druggists. PERRY DAVIS & SON, Mass. PROVIDENCE. R.I.

CHIMNEY ROCK ON THE PLATTE.

A wonder of nature: *Standing beside Chimney Rock, we felt no bigger than insects.*

Father says popular remedies such as this are "humbuggery." He gives calomel, laudanum, and mint tea for cholera, but his scientific treatments do not seem to gain better results.

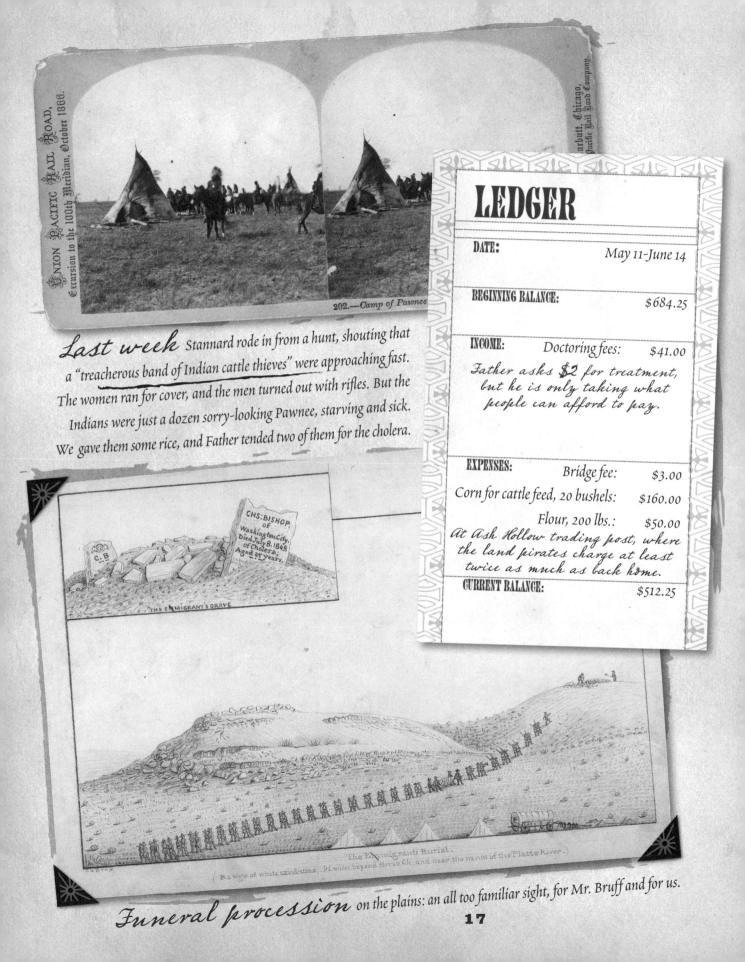

UNION PACIFIC RAIL ROAD, Excursion to the 100th Meridian, October 1866.

Barkutt, Chicago, Pacific Rail Road Company.

202.—Camp of Pawnee

Last week Stannard rode in from a hunt, shouting that a "treacherous band of Indian cattle thieves" were approaching fast. The women ran for cover, and the men turned out with rifles. But the Indians were just a dozen sorry-looking Pawnee, starving and sick. We gave them some rice, and Father tended two of them for the cholera.

LEDGER

DATE:	May 11–June 14
BEGINNING BALANCE:	$684.25
INCOME: Doctoring fees:	$41.00

Father asks $2 for treatment, but he is only taking what people can afford to pay.

EXPENSES: Bridge fee:	$3.00
Corn for cattle feed, 20 bushels:	$160.00
Flour, 200 lbs.:	$50.00

At Ash Hollow trading post, where the land pirates charge at least twice as much as back home.

CURRENT BALANCE:	$512.25

CHS: BISHOP of Washington City, Died July 8, 1849, of Cholera, Aged 25 Years.

C. B.

THE EMMIGRANT'S GRAVE

The Emmigrants Burial.
(Range of white sand-stone, 9 miles beyond Horse Cк. and near the banks of the Platte River.)

Funeral procession on the plains: an all too familiar sight, for Mr. Bruff and for us.

FORT LARAMIE

DATE: *June 20, 1852*

t Fort Laramie we camped for two days and barely saw Nathan all the while. He disappeared into the ramshackle huts of the traders that have bought themselves Indian brides from the local chieftains and settled around the fort. Most of the traders are mountain men who used to trap for fur in the Rockies. When beaver fur went out of fashion in Europe, they decided to trap desperate emigrants instead and charge them a fortune for supplies. That doesn't trouble Nathan's conscience in the least. Once again he is filling our ears full of numbers. He claims that chewing tobacco bought for 20 cents a pound in Santa Fe can be sold for $1 on the trail and $5 in Salt Lake City. Father is straining to keep him on the trail with us. We traded two rifles for some buffalo hides, as we are nearing the mountains, where it gets cold at night.

A Sioux brave offered to buy Abigail for ten fine horses. My father politely told him that white people do not sell women. The Sioux gestured to the traders and wondered why not, when at least some white men are willing to buy Indian brides.

The sutler here has luxuries we have not seen for many dusty miles. Abigail talked father into buying a jar of lemon syrup for $1.25. I purchased a 10-cent bottle of ink for 30 cents.

LEDGER

DATE:	June 14-20
BEGINNING BALANCE:	$512.25
INCOME:	$0

EXPENSES:

1 Jar lemon syrup:	$1.25
Ink:	$.30
5 Buffalo hides:	2 rifles

Barter is just as good as cash on the trail.

CURRENT BALANCE:	$510.70

Abigail has left her dresses in a heap and joined the third sex, leaving Mr. Strong to pray furiously she does not bring the cholera back. Byron is even more smitten than before.

The fort was the scene, last September, of a great tribal council. Indian chiefs from the Arapahos, Cheyennes, Sioux, Assiniboins, Snakes, Arikaras, Gros Ventres, and Crows agreed to keep peace on the trail and allow emigrants through unmolested. In exchange, the government agreed to give them $50,000 in goods every year.

INDEPENDENCE ROCK

DATE: *July 10, 1852*

We have finally left the Platte and the dread cholera behind. Yet each day yields plenty more to trouble us. Travel has been steep as we approach the mountains. A stubble of sagebrush covers the trail. There is grass here, but it is the first we have seen for miles, and the animals have eaten the corn we bought at Ash Hollow. Good drinking water is scarce. We still pass no fewer than five graves each day, and now we must add to it the stench of dead and dying cattle.

But all talk here is of the Sioux, who are said to be out for revenge. We are told that a party of braves took over a ferry outside Laramie, claiming it was rightfully theirs. A detachment of soldiers took it back, and one of the braves fired a shot before fleeing. The soldiers tracked down the Sioux and killed three of them. Byron tells me we have left Sioux territory and are in the domain of the Crow, but still we fear for our safety and for our cattle. At night we circle the wagons for protection.

A VIEW from
exhibiting the

Father addressed us all on this very spot, urging us not to lose hope. *"Nature has laid before you a stern test. Endure it and she will present you with all the fruits of a land unscarred by frost or drought."*

We climbed Independence Rock and wrote our names in axle grease alongside a thousand others. Byron and Abigail wrote theirs together.

Skinning a Buffalo

For Gods sake, do not drink, lest you lose your cattle as we have done.

LIFE ON THE TRAIL: A SURVIVAL GUIDE

DRINK CLEAN WATER

☞ Slap standing water to clear bugs before dipping.

☞ Place cloth over cup to strain dirt.

CLEAN LICE FROM CLOTHES

☞ Place over anthill to make a feast for the ants.

AVOID HAZARDS

☞ Read everything you see; your fellow travelers mean to be helpful.

When cattle die of starvation, we are eager to take what meat we can so we do not meet the same fate.

South Pass

July 15, 1852

We are encamped on the central ridge of the continent. Here are the first waters we have seen that flow to the West. Tomorrow we will follow them.

Father gathered his strength for some speechifying tonight. "We stand here at the summit of our lives, the past laid out to our east, the future to our west..." and so on.

I have sent several entries from my journal east with a mail wagon for 50 cents, though I am not optimistic they will ever arrive.

It is powerful cold here tonight and the peaks around us are painted with snow. I found Joseph chained to a wagon as Mr. Master fears he will run off. I offered him my buffalo hide, but he would not take it.

Mr. Strong and Father argued for some time tonight, and I found Abigail mad as a wet hen. It seems Mr. Strong says he will have no one "dressed in the devil's garments" shining up to his son. He is breaking with the company and moving ahead tomorrow.

We have circled the wagons each night to pen the cattle and allow the sentries to guard more effectively against the Sioux.

Stannard and his cronymen have refused guard duty since we left St. Joe. They prefer to gamble at cards, and they have found no shortage of makeshift games along the way.

LITTLE COLORADO DESERT

DATE: *July 20, 1852*

The oxen are gone, and we are in despair, thanks to a band of hostile Sioux. My brother saw it happen, but neither he nor anyone else could prevent it. Nathan and three other men from our company had driven the animals six miles off trail to find tolerably good grass for them to eat. As they were taking their noontime meal with the beasts, several young Indian braves rode headlong for the herd whooping and firing rifles in the air. The animals spooked and left their dining place at a full run. Nathan and the others ran for their horses, only to find that they too had been stolen. They could do nothing but watch as the oxen, our faithful guides to the West, disappeared into a cloud of dust toward the Green River.

Here is the toll taken by the Indian for our passage through his hunting ground.

Nathan rode a borrowed horse ahead to Green River, at Stannard's urging. Stannard's associates there have an abundance of cattle to sell, though the beasts are miserable specimens.

Nathan spent our last savings on four yoke of oxen and returned with a plan that I will reveal shortly.

Mother allowed herself to wonder aloud why we left comfortable circumstances in Springfield for this. But she gathered herself to press ahead. My family combined with another, which had no oxen to pull their wagon. Each family left half their belongings in a heap by the trail and set off in a single wagon.

Father, Mother, and Abigail will move on to Fort Hall while Nathan and I stay behind and attempt to rebuild our savings.

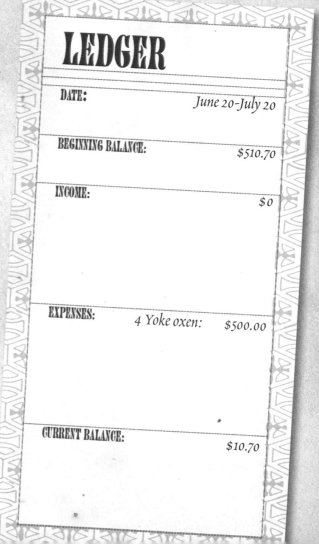

LEDGER	
DATE:	June 20–July 20
BEGINNING BALANCE:	$510.70
INCOME:	$0
EXPENSES: 4 Yoke oxen:	$500.00
CURRENT BALANCE:	$10.70

Green River Ferry

July 28, 1852

Here is Nathan's plan: The Reed Brothers Ferry.

The crossing is hazardous, and rumor has it that 40 souls lie buried in the banks downstream. This boy, who saved a yoke of oxen, was more fortunate. He lost only his pants and socks to the current.

We use the beds of two old wagons, lashed together and sealed with tar. We have hired a pilot to guide the ferry by rope and another to pole.

Stannard has stayed behind with the traders here. Some say these men burn grassland so emigrants will be obliged to sell their starving cattle cheap. The traders turn around and sell them to people like my mother and father, who in their desperation will pay any price.

Thomas Moor holds a charter from the Mormons, who claim the right to license ferry operators in these parts. We have set up downriver from Moor and are charging half the price.

Nathan earns extra money fixing wagon wheels after the ferry stops for the evening. I may have to bind him to a horse to get him away from this place.

FERRY

REED FERRY $6

LEDGER

DATE:	July 20-27
BEGINNING BALANCE:	$10.70

INCOME:

Ferry (135 wagons at $6 ea.):	$810.00
Ferry (320 animals at $.25 ea.):	$80.00
Blacksmithing:	$262.00

EXPENSES:

2 Ferry operators (5 days at $15/day ea.):	$150.00
Food and supplies:	$52.00

CURRENT BALANCE:	$960.70

GREEN RIVER

DATE: *July 28, 1852*

Nathan and I paid a visit to the trading post yesterday and discovered a suspicious sight: a healthy ox that bore a strong resemblance to Garrison. We investigated further, and I believe we have solved the mystery of our missing cattle and unmasked the "Indian" thieves. Here are the clues:

* An "R" branded onto another ox that looked suspiciously like Irving.

*  An Indian costume of buffalo hide and feathers, found on a noontime visit to Stannard's tent.

* A horse looking much like Nathan's, corralled with a dozen more behind the trading post.

The "Indians" who stampeded our livestock were none other than Stannard and his cronies, dressed for a costume ball. We are not sure what to do, as the traders are a rough lot and well armed. In the meantime, we had the Mormons to vex us.

We are in Utah Territory now, and it is run by the Mormons like a country. They maintain their own army, called the Nauvoo Legion.

This stern fellow is Brigham Young, the leader of the Mormons. He has led his followers west by the thousands to find a home where they can worship in peace. He told them to settle in a place no one else wanted, and so they built their capital, Salt Lake City, in a desert where the only water is spoiled by salt. The Mormons seem to be making the best of it. They do not own the trading post at Green River, but they have taken over ferry operations along this part of the trail. Like all the ferry operators from Kansas on out, they do not take kindly to competition, and we are not sure how long they will let us operate.

BRANLEY PASS

DATE: *August 7, 1852*

After riding hard for a day, we are bound for Fort Hall with cattle in tow, and here is how it happened. We decided not to anger the Mormons any longer but to take our revenge against the traders and be done with Green River. We packed our meager belongings and our earnings, leaving Nathan's smithy tools behind. Under cover of darkness, we stole back Nathan's horse and one other. We rode first to the east and left a message on the trail to warn unsuspecting emigrants of the scoundrels at Green River. Passing back through, we engaged in some trickery of our own, setting a dozen horses and a hundred head of cattle free to move on to Oregon or wherever they choose. By first light we were well along our way, driving Garrison, Irving, and six new oxen toward a reunion with our family.

EAST

BEWARE

WEST

LEDGER

DATE: July 27-Aug. 7

BEGINNING BALANCE: $960.70

INCOME:
Ferry (262 wagons at $6 ea.): $1,668.00
Ferry (828 animals at $.25 ea.): $207.00
Blacksmithing: $495.00

EXPENSES:
2 Ferry operators
(10 days at $15/day ea.): $300.00
Food and supplies: $60.00

CURRENT BALANCE: $2,970.70

Land or Lucre?

Flush with coin from our ferry operation, Nathan sa[ys]
wants to take the California Trail after Fort Hall and
to strike it rich in the gold fields. He says California is t[he]
place where men make real fortunes; in Oregon they merely
toil their lives away in obscurity. We debated by the fire, and
here, as I see it, are the arguments for both.

	FOR	AGAINST
CALIFORNIA 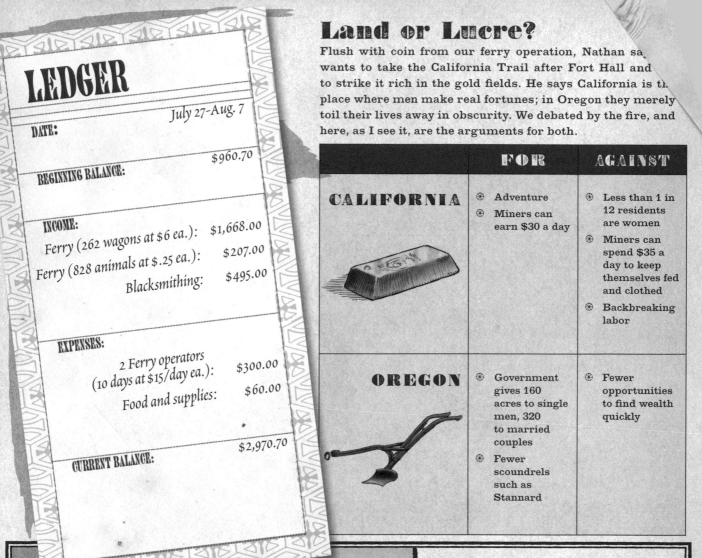	✳ Adventure ✳ Miners can earn $30 a day	✳ Less than 1 in 12 residents are women ✳ Miners can spend $35 a day to keep themselves fed and clothed ✳ Backbreaking labor
OREGON	✳ Government gives 160 acres to single men, 320 to married couples ✳ Fewer scoundrels such as Stannard	✳ Fewer opportunities to find wealth quickly

BEWARE THE WATER: A SURVIVAL GUIDE

☞ Many of the streams in these parts are poisoned with alkali, yet the cattle are so desperate we cannot keep them from drinking.

☞ Signs of alkali poisoning: swelling on stomach and chest, cough, death.

☞ Cure: Pour grease or water mixed with flour down the animal's throat.

FORT HALL

We arrived Fort Hall after a six-day journey driving the oxen from Green River. Father and Mother and Abigail were much relieved to see us. I thought that I noticed a tear even in Abigail's eye, but she composed herself quickly and informed us that accomodations at Fort Hall were inferior and we should have come earlier.

The reunion did not last long before we turned to more practical matters. We purchased a new wagon and gave the one we were sharing, including the old oxen, to the family Mother and Father had combined with. And so, we press on.

A man coming east had a supply of newspapers from Oregon City. We purchased one for 50 cents. I asked the man if he would consider my journal for publication. He laughed and said I would have to wait and ask the editor when we arrived.

Four days' ride from Fort Hall, we came across a great curiosity known as Soda Springs. Mixed with sugar, the water from the spring makes a drink equal to any soda prepared in Illinois. Some travelers found it a welcome distraction from the day's labors.

We saw this beside the trail just outside of Green River. Abigail has committed every word to memory.

Dear Abigail. We passed here July 20. Everyone well. Keep heart, we shall meet in Oregon City. Yrs Byron

INSIDE VIEW OF FORT HALL.

LEDGER

DATE:	July 27-Aug. 8
BEGINNING BALANCE:	$2,970.70
INCOME:	$0
EXPENSES:	Wagon: $200.00
	Flour, 30 lbs.: $15.00
CURRENT BALANCE:	$2,755.70

Dear Grandfather:

We have survived many adventures on the trail thus far. I am recording them all, and I wonder if you have seen my letters published in the newspaper. Nathan and I have spent a fortnight as ferry operators to recoup losses suffered when our cattle were stampeded. We are now rich in coin, but it is little use to us here. Fort Hall is an old boot, run down at the heel, and we are running short of supplies. We bought what little flour could be had, but it is not enough to sustain us to Oregon. What I wouldn't give for one of Mother's apple pies now. It is a hard life, but it is not comfort that has produced the great masterpieces of literature. It is good training indeed out here. I hope you will come join us when we are settled.

Yours,
William

CALIFORNIA JUNCTION

DATE: *August 13, 1852*

We reached the junction of the California Trail today, which was the occasion of much debate between the Oregonians and the gold hunters. Many farewells were said at the end of it all. One of them I will remember for the rest of my days. I was awake late in the night taking my turn as sentry when I was startled by a rustling in the sagebrush not 30 feet distant. I approached with nary a breath, expecting to be run through by a fierce arrowhead. Instead I came upon Joseph, huddled against the chill air. He did not start but told me with some trepidation that he was taking his freedom. He did not wish to dig gold for Mr. Master in California and was going to Oregon. I did not hesitate but told him to wait. I went to the wagon and returned with a buffalo hide and $50 in coin. This time he took it willingly and disappeared into the night. I returned to my duties as guard, feeling that I had done the first thing of importance in my 15 years.

Oregon-bound emigrants are held to be a better lot than the ruffians bound for the mines. It is said (falsely) that a pile of gold-bearing quartz points the way to California so as not to overwork the miner's brain.

34

The slave masters post ads like this one when their "property" escapes. Thanks to the Fugitive Slave Law passed two years ago, I could be jailed for helping Joseph to freedom, even though slavery is not allowed in Oregon.

$200 Reward.

RANAWAY from the subscriber, on the night of Thursday, the 30th of Sepember.

FIVE NEGRO SLAVES,

To-wit: one Negro man, his wife, and three children.
The man is a black negro, full height, very erect, his face a little thin. He is about forty years of age, and calls himself *Washington Reed*, and is known by the name of Washington. He is probably well dressed, possibly takes with him an ivory headed cane, and is of good address. Several of his teeth are gone.
Mary, his wife, is about thirty years of age, a bright mulatto woman, and quite stout and strong.
The oldest of the children is a boy, of the name of FIELDING, twelve years of age, a dark mulatto, with heavy eyelids. He probably wore a new cloth cap.
MATILDA, the second child, is a girl, six years of age, rather a dark mulatto, but a bright and smart looking child.
MALGOLM, the youngest, is a boy, four years old, a lighter mulatto than the last, and about equally as bright. He probably also wore a cloth cap. If examined, he will be found to have a swelling at the navel.
Washington and Mary have lived at or near St. Louis, with the subscriber, for about 15 years.
It is supposed that they are making their way to Chicago, and that a white man accompanies them, that they will travel chiefly at night, and most probably in a covered wagon.
A reward of $150 will be paid for their apprehension, so that I can get them, if taken within one hundred miles of St. Louis, and $200 if taken beyond that, and secured so that I can get them, and other reasonable additional charges, if delivered to the subscriber, or to THOMAS ALLEN, Esq., at St. Louis, Mo. The above negroes, for the last few years, have been in possession of Thomas Allen, Esq., of St. Louis.

WM. RUSSELL.

ST. LOUIS, Oct. 1, 1847.

Nathan is staying with us all the way to Oregon after being cornered by Father for some hours. Father let Nathan know, quite eloquently, that he might as well play roulette as dig for gold and that Oregon is where people make an honest living. If Father's speeches made Nathan stay, it is certainly the first time they did more than add warm breeze to the air at supper time.

THREE ISLAND CROSSING

DATE: *August 26, 1852*

I **am cold** and hungry and tired, but I am alive, and for that I am in debt to an unlikely savior. It is a treacherous crossing here, a wide expanse of the Snake with a rushing current, broken by three islands. We hired three guides from the Shoshone tribe to help us ford, and all was going well until we reached the midpoint between the last island and the shore. One of the lead oxen found a hole and lost his footing. He panicked the others, and they turned abruptly downstream. Father and Nathan lay abed in the wagon, stricken by mountain fever. I did not think of the churning river but acted without thought. I plunged into the water and tried to turn the oxen back, but I too lost my footing, and the river swept me into a maelstrom. I gasped for air. The current pulled me down. The more I fought, the more the river tightened its grip, until finally I gave in and let the water take me, thinking I would come to rest either in Oregon or in God's heaven. Instead, I found myself in the embrace of one of our Shoshone guides. He dragged me ashore while his companions saved our wagon.

Chief Washakie of the Shoshone is known to be a friend to the emigrants. He has counseled his people to keep peace with us, and we are particularly grateful tonight.

We traded clothing and ammunition for salmon, and it caused me to reflect upon the value we assign to our possessions. At home in Springfield, where food was plentiful, were a man to offer me a hunk of fish for my best shirt, I would have considered him a thief. Here, I consider him my savior.

A Shoshone woman
taught mother a new delicacy: Herd
crickets into firepits and roast them until
they burst. Mash and mix with roots and
herbs to make flat cakes for baking. I closed
my eyes and tried to imagine apple pie.

W.H.JACKS

Here is where our
journey nearly ended.

August 4. Abigail,
only the miles keep us
apart. We are together
in my heart, Byron.

Yes, another.

Grande Ronde Valley

September 12, 1852.

What a welcome sight is this valley, a true oasis in the desert. There is fine, cool water to drink and grass for the cattle.

We found some provisions here, but not many. Nathan is full of plans to purchase supplies when we arrive in Oregon and bring them back here to sell at a great profit next year.

We will not linger long here. The snowcapped peaks ahead are beautiful but warn of great danger to come if we do not hurry.

The descent from the mountains was treacherous as any we have made. We kept the wheels locked the entire way, and still we needed several men to steady each wagon with ropes.

The Indians here want for nothing. They cultivate the fields and own the finest ponies I have seen. Many have been educated by Methodist missionaries and speak tolerable English.

LEDGER

DATE:	Aug. 8–Sept. 12
BEGINNING BALANCE:	$2,755.70

INCOME:

Doctoring fees:	$16.00

Few travelers have any money left to pay.

EXPENSES:

Flour, 50 lbs.:	$20.00
Beef, 20 lbs.:	$10.00

CURRENT BALANCE:	$2,741.70

THE DALLES
(CAMP DRUM)

DATE: *October 1, 1852*

I can scarcely believe it true, but the trail ends for us here. We have been four months in the barren wilds with a handful of tents, tipis, and forts posing as homes. The Dalles, or Camp Drum, as the army calls it, consists of a store, a barracks, a Catholic mission, and, miracle of miracles, HOUSES. They are little more than shacks with dirt floors, but to me they are water glimmering in the desert. I would like nothing better than to take up residence here and settle for the rest of my days. Alas, we are not through yet. Mount Hood looms like a white-crested battlement, barring the way to paradise. The women and I are strong, but Father and Nathan still suffer. We are selling the oxen (for next to nothing) and taking the Columbia—the last churning river—to our final destination.

PICKLES

The scurvy has taken hold, as we have not seen a berry for miles, and all dried fruit was consumed long ago. Father has treated people with his treasured pickles, and they are a miraculous cure.

And still another.

Oct. 1. Abigail, look for me in Portland city. I will wait for you there till I am old. Yours always, Byron.